St John Passion

Bob Chilcott

for soloists, SATB chorus, and small ensemble or organ
(with opt. cello)

vocal score

MUSIC DEPARTMENT

OXFORD
UNIVERSITY PRESS

OXFORD
UNIVERSITY PRESS

Great Clarendon Street, Oxford OX2 6DP,
United Kingdom

Oxford University Press is a department of the University of Oxford.
It furthers the University's aim of excellence in research, scholarship,
and education by publishing worldwide. Oxford is a registered trade mark of
Oxford University Press in the UK and in certain other countries

© Oxford University Press 2013

Bob Chilcott has asserted his right under the Copyright, Designs
and Patents Act, 1988, to be identified as the Composer of this Work

First published 2013

ISBN 978-0-19-339759-0

Music origination by
Enigma Music Production Services, Amersham, Bucks.

Printed in Great Britain on acid-free paper by
Halstan & Co. Ltd, Amersham, Bucks.

Contents

Scoring

The *St John Passion* is scored for SATB chorus and the following soloists:

Evangelist (tenor)
Jesus (baritone)
Pilate (baritone)
Soprano
Woman (soprano)
Peter (tenor)
Officer (tenor)
Servant (tenor)

The smaller solo roles (Woman, Peter, Officer, Servant), and if needed even the larger parts of Pilate and Jesus and the soprano solo in the meditations, may be taken by members of the chorus.

The five hymn settings are intended for performance by the audience/congregation in addition to the choir. The melodies are printed with the texts on p. vi–xii.

Instrumentation

The accompaniment to this work exists in two versions:

1. For small ensemble

horn in F
2 trumpets in B flat
trombone
tuba
timpani
viola
cello
organ (using the part available on hire/rental)

Full scores, vocal scores, and instrumental parts are available on hire/rental from the publisher's Hire Library or appropriate agent.

2. For organ and optional cello

The organist plays from the vocal score. The cello solos in Part 3 (pp. 61–2, 68, 69–70, and 77) may be performed on the organ or, preferably, by a cello soloist. A separate cello part is printed on pp. 82–3.

Composer's note

My setting of the Passion is an hour-long work telling the story of Christ's trial and Crucifixion using the text from St John's Gospel. It was written specially for Matthew Owens and the Choir of Wells Cathedral for performance within a Cathedral Service on Palm Sunday, 23 March 2013. The work is scored for soprano, tenor, and two baritone soloists, mixed choir, solo viola and cello, brass quintet, organ, and timpani.

As in the great Passion settings by J. S. Bach, the story is narrated by a tenor Evangelist. I have designed the narrative to be sung in an arioso style that gains momentum as the drama unfolds. The solo roles in the narrative are identified with specific instruments from the ensemble: the Evangelist is accompanied by the viola and cello, Pilate by two trumpets, and Jesus by horn, trombone, tuba, and organ. The role of the choir within the narrative is to play the part of the crowd or a group of soldiers who comment from time to time in short outbursts. The larger role for the choir is the singing of four meditations that punctuate various points in the drama. I have tried in these meditations to emulate the style of a strophic carol in the mould of a writer such as Thomas Ravenscroft, cast in a simple, melodic way. The texts are taken from English poems from the thirteenth to the early seventeenth centuries that express deeply human responses to death, to life, and to man's relationship with the world and with God. Two of these meditations are sung by the choir with soprano solo, the last of which ('Jesus, my Leman') expresses most poignantly the human response to seeing Christ crucified on the Cross. I have also set five well-known Passiontide hymn texts ('It is a thing most wonderful', 'Drop, drop, slow tears', 'Jesu, grant me this, I pray', 'There is a green hill far away', and 'When I survey the Wondrous Cross'), which are designed to be sung by the choir and audience/congregation together.

I was fortunate as a singer to perform the Evangelist role in both the great Passions of Bach a number of times. I also remember as a boy chorister in King's College, Cambridge, singing the simpler Renaissance versions of the Passion chanted by the Dean and Chaplain of the Chapel in Holy Week. It is the austerity, the agony, and ultimately the grace of this story that has inspired me to write this piece, which was performed for the first time in a magnificent building where this same story has been commemorated for almost a thousand years.

Duration: *c.*55 minutes

This note may be reproduced as required for programme notes.

Texts

These texts and melodies may be reproduced as required for programme notes and to allow audience/congregation participation in the hymns during a performance of the *St John Passion*.

1. Sing, my tongue, the glorious battle

Bishop Venantius Fortunatus (c.530–c.600), trans. Percy Dearmer (1867–1936)

Sing, my tongue, the glorious battle,
Sing the ending of the fray;
Now above the Cross, the trophy,
Sound the loud triumphant lay:
Tell how Christ, the world's Redeemer,
As a victim won the day.

God in pity saw man fallen,
Shamed and sunk in misery,
When he fell on death by tasting
Fruit of the forbidden tree;
Then another tree was chosen
Which the world from death should free.

2. The Garden

John 18: 1, 3–13

Jesus went forth with his disciples over the brook Cedron, where was a garden, into the which he entered, and his disciples. Judas then, having received a band of men and officers from the chief priests and Pharisees, cometh thither with lanterns and torches and weapons. Jesus therefore, knowing all things that should come upon him, went forth, and said unto them, Whom seek ye? They answered him, Jesus of Nazareth. Jesus saith unto them, I am he. And Judas also, which betrayed him, stood with them. And soon then as he had said unto them, I am he, they went backward, and fell to the ground. Then asked he them again, Whom seek ye? And they said, Jesus of Nazareth. Jesus answered, I have told you that I am he: if therefore ye seek me, let these go their way: That the saying might be fulfilled, which he spake, Of them which thou gavest me have I lost none. Then Simon Peter having a sword drew it, and smote the high priest's servant, and cut off his right ear. The servant's name was Malchus. Then said Jesus unto Peter, Put up thy sword into the sheath: the cup which my Father hath given me, shall I not drink it? Then the band and the captain and officers of the Jews took Jesus, and bound him, And led him away to Annas first; for he was the father in law to Caiaphas, which was the high priest that same year.

3. Hymn: It is a thing most wonderful

Music: Bob Chilcott; Words: Bishop William Walsham How (1823–97)

1. It is a thing most wonderful,
   Almost too wonderful to be,
   That God's own Son should come from heav'n
   And die to save a child, a child like me.

2. And yet I know that it is true;
   He chose a poor and humble lot,
   And wept and toiled and mourned and died,
   For love of those who loved, who loved him not.

3. It is most wonderful to know
   His love for me so free and sure;
   But 'tis more wonderful to see
   My love for him so faint, so faint and poor.

4. Peter's Denial

John 18: 14–27

Now Caiaphas was he, which gave counsel to the Jews, that it was expedient that one man should die for the people. And Simon Peter followed Jesus, and so did another disciple: that disciple was known unto the high priest, and went in with Jesus into the palace of the high priest. But Peter stood at the door without. Then went out that other disciple, which was known unto the high priest, and spake unto her that kept the door, and brought in Peter. Then saith the damsel that kept the door unto Peter, Art not thou also one of this man's disciples? He saith, I am not. And the servants and officers stood there, who had made a fire of coals; for it was cold: and they warmed themselves: and Peter stood with them, and warmed himself. The high priest then asked Jesus of his disciples, and of his doctrine. Jesus answered him, I spake openly to the world; I ever taught in the synagogue, and in the temple, whither the Jews always resort; and in secret have I said nothing. Why askest thou me? Ask them which heard me, what I have said unto them: behold, they know what I said. And when he had thus spoken, one of the officers which stood by struck Jesus with the palm of his hand, saying, Answerest thou the high priest so? Jesus answered him, If I have spoken evil, bear witness of the evil: but if well, why smitest thou me? Now Annas had sent him bound unto Caiaphas the high priest. And Simon Peter stood and warmed himself. They said therefore unto him, Art not thou also one of his disciples? He denied it, and said, I am not. One of the servants of the high priest, being his kinsman whose ear Peter cut off, saith, Did not I see thee in the garden with him? Peter then denied again: and immediately the cock crew.

5. Meditation: Miserere, my Maker

Anon., c.1615

Miserere, my Maker,
O have mercy on me, wretch, strangely distressèd,
Cast down with sin oppressèd;
Mightily vexed to the soul's bitter anguish,
E'en to the death I languish.
Yet let it please Thee
To hear my ceaseless crying:
Miserere, miserere, I am dying.

Miserere, my Saviour,
I, alas, am for my sins fearfully grievèd,
And cannot be relievèd
But by Thy death, which Thou didst suffer for me,
Wherefore I adore Thee.
And do beseech Thee
To hear my ceaseless crying:
Miserere, miserere, I am dying.

Holy Spirit, miserere,
Comfort my distressèd soul, grieved for youth's folly,
Purge, cleanse and make it holy;
With Thy sweet due of grace and peace inspire me,
How I desire Thee.
And strengthen me now
In this, my ceaseless crying:
Miserere, miserere, I am dying.

6. Hymn: Drop, drop, slow tears

Music: Bob Chilcott; Words: Phineas Fletcher (1582–1650)

SHERLAW-JOHNSON

1. Drop, drop, slow tears,
   And bathe those beauteous feet,
   Which brought from heav'n
   The news and Prince of Peace.

2. Cease not, wet eyes,
   His mercies to entreat;
   To cry for vengeance
   Sin doth never cease.

3. In your deep floods
   Drown all my faults and fears;
   Nor let his eye
   See sin, but through my tears.

7. The Judgment Hall (I)

John 18: 28–36

Then led they Jesus from Caiaphas unto the hall of judgment: and it was early; and they themselves went not into the judgment hall, lest they should be defiled; but that they might eat the passover. Pilate then went out unto them, and said, What accusation bring ye against this man? They answered and said unto him, If he were not a malefactor, we would not have delivered him up unto thee. Then said Pilate unto them, Take ye him, and judge him according to your law. The Jews therefore said unto him, It is not lawful for us to put any man to death: That the saying of Jesus might be fulfilled, which he spake, signifying what death he should die. Then Pilate entered into the judgment hall again, and called Jesus, and said unto him, Art thou the King of the Jews? Jesus answered him, Sayest thou this thing of thyself, or did others tell it thee of me? Pilate answered, Am I a Jew? Thine own nation and the chief priests have delivered thee unto me: what hast thou done? Jesus answered, My kingdom is not of this world: if my kingdom were of this world, then would my servants fight, that I should not be delivered to the Jews: but now is my kingdom not from hence.

8. Hymn: Jesu, grant me this, I pray

Music: Bob Chilcott; Words: 17th-century Latin, trans. Sir Henry Williams Baker (1821–77)

WITHAMS

1. Jesu, grant me this, I pray,
   Ever in thy heart to stay;
   Let me evermore abide
   Hidden in thy wounded side.

2. If the evil one prepare,
   Or the world, a tempting snare,
   I am safe when I abide
   In thy heart and wounded side.

3. If the flesh, more dangerous still,
   Tempt my soul to deeds of ill,
   Naught I fear when I abide
   In thy heart and wounded side.

4. Death will come one day to me;
   Jesu, cast me not from thee:
   Dying let me still abide
   In thy heart and wounded side.

9. Meditation: Christ, my Beloved

William Baldwin (d. c.1563)

Christ, my Beloved which still doth feed
Among the flowers, having delight
Among his faithful lilies,
Doth take great care for me indeed,
And I again with all my might
Will do what so his will is.

My Love in me and I in him,
Conjoined by love, will still abide
Among the faithful lilies
Till day do break, and truth do dim
All shadows dark and cause them slide,
According as his will is.

10. The Judgment Hall (II)

John 18: 37–19: 11

Pilate therefore said unto him, Art thou a king then? Jesus answered, Thou sayest that I am a king. To this end was I born, and for this cause came I into the world, that I should bear witness unto the truth. Every one that is of the truth heareth my voice. Pilate saith unto him, What is truth? And when he said this, he went out again unto the Jews, and saith unto them, I find in him no fault at all. But ye have a custom, that I should release unto you one at the passover: will ye therefore that I release unto you the King of the Jews? Then cried they all again, saying, Not this man, but Barabbas. Now Barabbas was a robber. Then Pilate therefore took Jesus, and scourged him. And the soldiers platted a crown of thorns, and put it on his head, and they put on him a purple robe, And said, Hail, King of the Jews! And they smote him with their hands. Pilate therefore went forth again, and saith unto them, Behold, I bring him forth to you, that ye may know that I find no fault in him. Then came Jesus forth, wearing the crown of thorns, and the purple robe, And Pilate saith unto them, Behold the man! When the chief priests therefore and officers saw him, they cried out, saying, Crucify him, crucify him. Pilate saith unto them, Take ye him, and crucify him: for I find no fault in him. The Jews answered him, We have a law, and by our law he ought to die, because he made himself the Son of God. When Pilate therefore heard that saying, he was the more afraid; And went again into the judgment hall, and saith unto Jesus, Whence art thou? But Jesus gave him no answer. Then saith Pilate unto him, Speakest thou not unto me? Knowest thou not that I have power to crucify thee, and have power to release thee? Jesus answered, Thou couldest have no power at all against me, except it were given thee from above: therefore he that delivered me unto thee hath the greater sin.

11. Meditation: Away vain world

Alexander Montgomerie (?1545–?1610), modernized and adapted by Bob Chilcott

Away vain world, bewitcher of my heart!
My sorrow shows, my sin makes me to smart!
Yet will I not despair
But to my God repair,
He has mercy ay,
Therefore will I pray.
He has mercy ay and loves me
Though by his humbling hand he proves me.

Once more away, shows loth[1] the world to leave,
Bids oft adieu with it that holds me slave.
Loth am I to forgo
This sweet alluring foe.
Since thy ways are vain,
Shall I thee retain?
Since thy ways are vain, I quite[2] thee.
Thy pleasures shall no more delight me.

What shall I say? Are all my pleasures past?
Shall worldly joys now take their leave at last?
Yea, Christ, these earthly toys
Shall turn in heavenly joys.
Let the world be gone,
I'll love Christ alone!
Let the world be gone, I care not.
Christ is my love alone, I fear not.

[1] loth = loath/unwilling
[2] quite = quit/leave

12. Jesus is Crucified

John 19: 12–22

And from thenceforth Pilate sought to release him: but the Jews cried out, saying, If thou let this man go, thou art not Caesar's friend: whosoever maketh himself a king speaketh against Caesar. When Pilate therefore heard that saying, he brought Jesus forth, and sat down in the judgment seat in a place that is called the Pavement, but in the Hebrew, Gabbatha. And it was the preparation of the passover, and about the sixth hour: and he saith unto the Jews, Behold your King! But they cried out, Away with him, away with him, crucify him. Pilate saith unto them, Shall I crucify your King? The chief priests answered, We have no king but Caesar. Then delivered he him therefore unto them to be crucified. And they took Jesus, and led him away. And he bearing his cross went forth into a place called the place of a skull, which is called in the Hebrew Golgotha: Where they crucified him, and two other with him, on either side one, and Jesus in the midst. And Pilate wrote a title, and put it on the cross. And the writing was, JESUS OF NAZARETH THE KING OF THE JEWS. This title then read many of the Jews: for the place where Jesus was crucified was nigh to the city: and it was written in Hebrew, and Greek, and Latin. Then said the chief priests of the Jews to Pilate, Write not, The King of the Jews; but that he said, I am King of the Jews. Pilate answered, What I have written I have written.

13. Hymn: There is a green hill far away

Music: Bob Chilcott; Words: Mrs Cecil Frances Alexander (1818–95)

© Oxford University Press 2013

1. There is a green hill far away,
   Without a city wall,
   Where the dear Lord was crucified,
   Who died to save us all,
   Who died to save us all.

2. We may not know, we cannot tell,
   What pains he had to bear,
   But we believe it was for us
   He hung and suffered there,
   He hung and suffered there.

3. He died that we might be forgiv'n,
   He died to make us good,
   That we might go at last to heav'n,
   Saved by his precious blood,
   Saved by his precious blood.

4. O dearly, dearly has he loved,
   And we must love him too,
   And trust in his redeeming blood,
   And try his works to do,
   And try his works to do.

14. The Crucifixion

John 19: 23–7

Then the soldiers, when they had crucified Jesus, took his garments, and made four parts, to every soldier a part; and also his coat: now the coat was without seam, woven from the top throughout. They said therefore among themselves, Let us not rend it, but cast lots for it, whose it shall be: That the scripture might be fulfilled, which saith, They parted my raiment among them, and for my vesture they did cast lots. These things therefore the soldiers did. Now there stood by the cross of Jesus his mother, and his mother's sister, Mary the wife of Cleophas, and Mary Magdalene. When Jesus therefore saw his mother, and the disciple standing by, whom he loved, he saith unto his mother, Woman, behold thy son! Then saith he to the disciple, Behold thy mother!

15. Meditation: Jesus, my Leman

13th-century English, adapted by Bob Chilcott

When I see upon the Cross
Jesus, my leman[1],
And by him standing Mary and Johan,
With his back scourged
And his side pierced,
For the love of man,
Well ought I to weep
And sins relinquish,
If I know of love.

[1] leman = loved one

16. Jesus Dies on the Cross

John 19: 28–30

After this, Jesus knowing that all things were now accomplished, that the scripture might be fulfilled, saith, I thirst. Now there was set a vessel full of vinegar; and they filled a sponge with vinegar, and put it upon hyssop, and put it to his mouth. When Jesus had received the vinegar, he said, It is finished. And he bowed his head, and gave up the ghost.

17. Hymn: When I survey the Wondrous Cross

Music: Bob Chilcott; Words: Isaac Watts (1674–1748)

1. When I survey the Wondrous Cross,
   On which the Prince of glory died,
   My richest gain I count but loss,
   And pour contempt on all my pride,
   And pour contempt on all my pride.

2. Forbid it, Lord, that I should boast,
   Save in the death of Christ my God;
   All the vain things that charm me most,
   I sacrifice them to his blood,
   I sacrifice them to his blood.

3. See from his head, his hands, his feet,
   Sorrow and love flow mingled down;
   Did e'er such love and sorrow meet,
   Or thorns compose so rich a crown,
   Or thorns compose so rich a crown?

4. Were the whole realm of nature mine,
   That were a present far too small;
   Love so amazing, so divine,
   Demands my soul, my life, my all,
   Demands my soul, my life, my all.

St John Passion

ST JOHN PASSION

PART 1

1. Sing, my tongue, the glorious battle

Bishop Venantius Fortunatus (*c*.530–*c*.600)
trans. Percy Dearmer (1867–1936)

BOB CHILCOTT

1. Sing, my tongue, the glorious battle, Sing the ending of the fray;
2. God in pity saw man fallen, Shamed and sunk in misery,

Printed in Great Britain

OXFORD UNIVERSITY PRESS, MUSIC DEPARTMENT, GREAT CLARENDON STREET, OXFORD OX2 6DP
The Moral Rights of the Composer have been asserted. Photocopying this copyright material is ILLEGAL.

Now a-bove the Cross, the tro-phy, Sound the loud tri - um - phant lay:
When he fell on death by tast - ing Fruit of the for - bid - den tree;

Tell how Christ, the world's Re - deem - er, As a vic - tim won the
Then an - o - ther tree was cho - sen Which the world from death should

1.
day.

2.
free.

2. The Garden

John 18: 1, 3–13

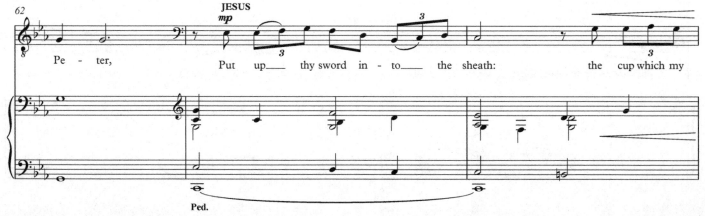

more agitated

EVANGELIST

Fa - ther hath gi - ven me, shall I not drink it, drink it? Then the

band and the cap - tain and of - fi - cers of the Jews took Je - sus, and

bound him, And led him a - way to An - nas first; for he was the fa - ther in

law to Ca - ia - phas, which was the high priest that same year.

poco rit.

3. Hymn: It is a thing most wonderful

Bishop William Walsham How (1823–97)

'ELTON'

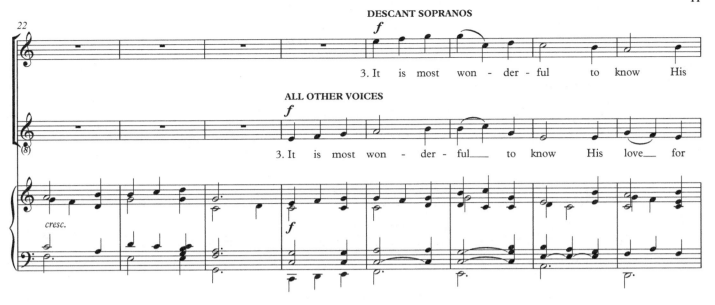

DESCANT SOPRANOS

3. It is most won-der-ful to know His

ALL OTHER VOICES

3. It is most won-der-ful to know His love for

love for me so free and sure; But 'tis more won-der-

me so free and sure; But 'tis more won-der-ful to

poco rit.

-ful to see My love for him so faint and poor.

see My love for him so faint, so faint and poor.

poco rit.

4. Peter's Denial

John 18: 14–27

world; I ev - er taught in the sy - na - gogue, and in the tem - ple,

whi - ther the Jews al - ways re - sort; and in se - cret have I said no - thing. Why

ask - est thou me? Ask them which heard me, what I have said un - to them: be -

Tempo I (♩ = *c.* 84)

EVANGELIST

- hold, they know what I said. And when he had thus spo - ken, one of the

Man.

He de-nied it, and said, I am not.

Man.

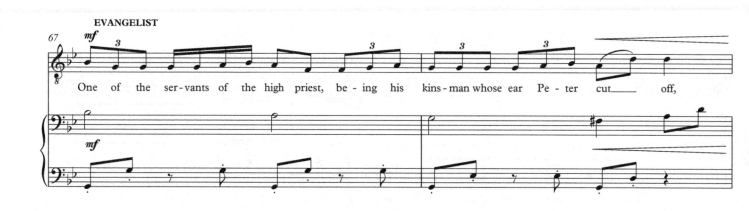

One of the ser-vants of the high priest, be-ing his kins-man whose ear Pe-ter cut___ off,

poco rit.   **Tempo II** (♩ = c.60)

saith, Did not I see thee in the gar-den with him? Pe-ter then de-nied a-

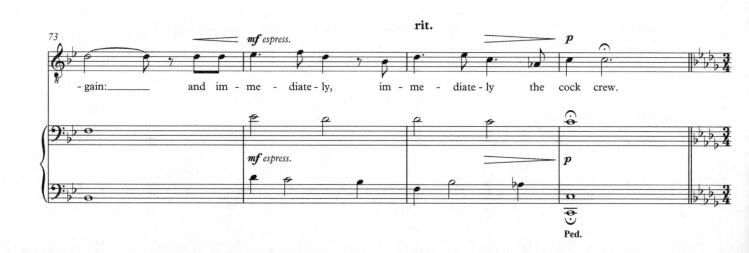

rit.

-gain:___ and im-me-diate-ly, im-me-diate-ly the cock crew.

Ped.

5. Meditation: Miserere, my Maker

Anon., *c.*1615

6. Hymn: Drop, drop, slow tears

Phineas Fletcher (1582–1650)

'SHERLAW-JOHNSON'

*Melody by Orlando Gibbons (1583–1625)

PART 2

7. The Judgment Hall (I)

John 18: 28–36

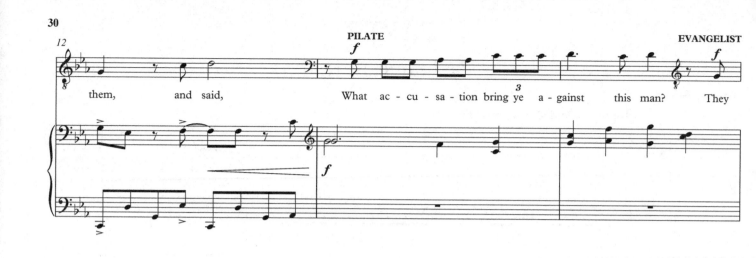

Then said Pi - late un - to them,

Take ye him, and

Man.

(PILATE) judge him ac - cord - ing to your law.

EVANGELIST

The Jews__ there - fore said un - to him,

S. A. It T. B.

Ped.

is not law - ful for us, for us to__ put__ a - ny man__ to death:

ff marcato

calmer

JESUS

Say - est thou this thing of thy - self, or did o - thers tell it thee of me?

more agitated

EVANGELIST

Pi - late an - swered,

PILATE

Am I a Jew? Thine own na - tion and the chief priests have de - li - vered thee un - to me: what hast thou done?

slowing

EVANGELIST

Je - sus an - swered,

calmer

My____ king - dom is not of this world: if my

king - dom were___ of this world, then would my ser - vants fight,

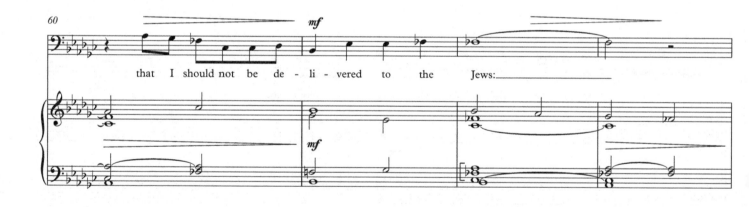

that I should not be de - li - vered to the Jews:____

rit.

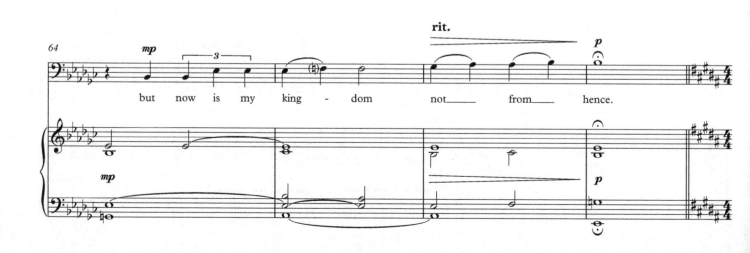

but now is my king - dom not___ from___ hence.

8. Hymn: *Jesu, grant me this, I pray*

17th-century Latin
trans. Sir Henry Williams Baker (1821–77)

'WITHAMS'

4. Death will come one day to me; Je - su, cast me
not from thee: Dy - ing let me still a - bide
In thy heart and wound - ed side.

9. Meditation: Christ, my Beloved

William Baldwin (d. *c*.1563)

10. The Judgment Hall (II)

John 18: 37–19: 11

you, that ye may know that I find no fault in him. Then came

Je - sus forth, Je - sus forth, wear-ing the crown of thorns, and the

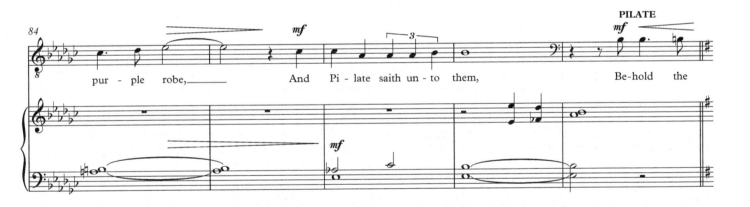

pur - ple robe,_____ And Pi - late saith un - to them, Be-hold the

man! When the

94 chief priests there-fore and of-fi-cers saw him, they cried out, say - ing,

98 Cru - ci - fy him, cru - ci - fy him, cru - ci - fy him.

102 EVANGELIST
Pi - late saith un-to them,

PILATE
Take ye him, and cru - ci - fy him: for I

Man.

107 find no fault in him.

EVANGELIST
The Jews

123

128

EVANGELIST
mp

When Pi-late there-fore heard that say-ing, he was the

mf dim.

mp

Man.

133

mf

more a-fraid;_____ And went a-gain in-to the judg-ment hall, and saith un-to

mf

mf

137

PILATE
f   *f*

Je-sus,   Whence art thou?

EVANGELIST
mp

But Je-sus gave him no an-swer.

f

mp

142

mf

Then saith Pi-late un-to him,

PILATE
f

Speak-est thou not un-to

mf

f

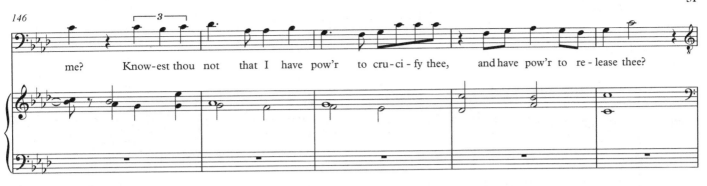

me? Know-est thou not that I have pow'r to cru-ci-fy thee, and have pow'r to re-lease thee?

poco rit. | **Slower** ♩ = c.54

EVANGELIST *mf*

JESUS *mp espress.*

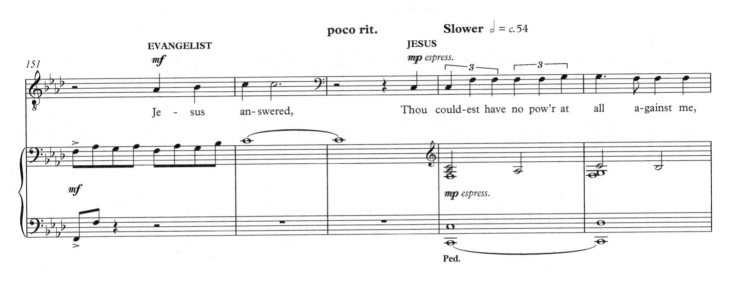

Je - sus an-swered, Thou could-est have no pow'r at all a-gainst me,

Ped.

ex - cept it were gi-ven___ thee___ from a - bove: there - fore

rit. | *dim.* | *p*

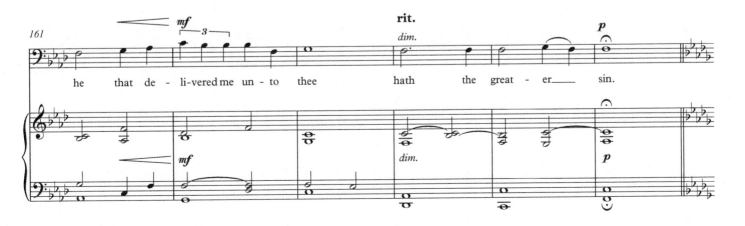

he that de - li-vered me un - to thee hath the great - er___ sin.

11. Meditation: Away vain world

Alexander Montgomerie (?1545–?1610)
modernized BC

to my God re-pair, He has mer-cy ay, There-fore will I pray.

God re-pair, He has mer-cy ay, will I pray.

to my God re-pair, He has mer-cy ay, There-fore will I pray.

God re-pair, He has mer-cy ay, will I pray.

He has mer-cy ay and loves me Though by his hum-bling hand he proves me. A - way,

Mer - cy, and loves me, by his hand. A - way, a -

He has mer-cy ay and loves me, by his hand. A - way, a -

Mer - cy, and loves me, by his hand. A - way,

Once more a - way, shows loth* the world to leave, Bids oft__ a - dieu with

- way,__ a - way,__ a - way, a - way,__ a - way, a - way, a -

- way, a - way,__ a - way, a - way, a - way,__ a - way, a -

a - way, a - way, a - way, a - way,

it that holds me slave._____ Loth am I to for - go This sweet al - lur - ing foe.

- way,__ a - way._____ Loth am I to for - go__ al - lur - ing foe.__

- way, a - way._____ Loth am I to for - go This sweet al - lur - ing foe.

a - - way._____ Loth am I to for - go al - lur - ing foe.

*loth = loath/unwilling

quite = quit/leave

shall I___ say? Are all my plea-sures past? Shall world-ly___ joys now take their leave at last?_____ Yea,

a - way, a - way,___ a - way, a - way, a - way,___ a - way,_____ Yea,

a - way, a - way, a - way,___ a - way, a - way, a - way,_____ Yea,

a - way, a - way, a - way, a - way,_____ Yea,

Christ, these earth-ly toys Shall turn in heav'n-ly joys. Let the world be gone, I'll love_ Christ a-lone!

Christ, these earth-ly toys___ in heav'n - ly joys.___ Let the world be gone,_ I'll love_ Christ a-lone!

Christ, these earth-ly toys Shall turn in heav'n-ly joys. Let the world be gone, I'll love_ Christ a - lone!_____

Christ, these earth-ly toys in heav'n - ly joys. Let the world be gone, I'll love Christ a-lone!

PART 3

12. *Jesus is Crucified*

John 19: 12–22

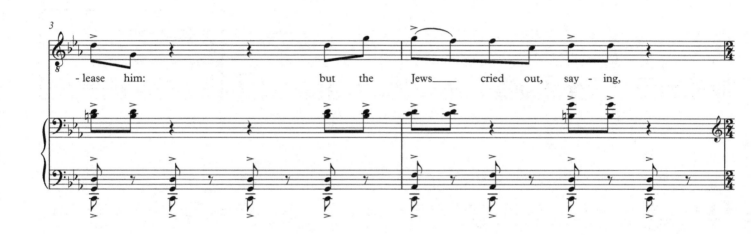

who - so - ev - er ma - keth him-self a king speak - eth a - gainst Cae - sar.

EVANGELIST

When Pi - late there-fore heard that say - ing, he brought Je - sus forth, and sat down in the

judg-ment seat in a place that is called the Pave - ment, but in the He-brew, Gab - ba - tha. And

Man.

*The bracketed section may be performed by a solo cellist. See p. 82 for a separate cello part.

two o-ther with him, on ei-ther side__ one, and Je-sus in the midst. And

Pi-late wrote a ti-tle, and put it on the cross.__ And the writ-ing was,__

JE - SUS OF NA-ZA-RETH THE KING__ OF THE JEWS.__ This

a little quicker

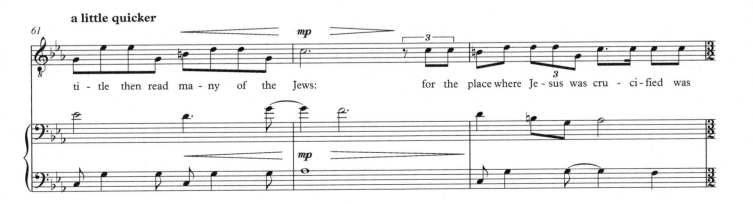

ti-tle then read ma-ny of the Jews: for the place where Je-sus was cru-ci-fied was

64

night to the city: and it was writ-ten in He-brew, and Greek, and

La - tin. Then said the chief priests of the Jews to Pi - late,

S.
A.

Write not, The King of the Jews; but that he said, I am King of the Jews.

T.
B.

Ped.

EVANGELIST   PILATE

Pi - late an - swered, What I have writ-ten I have writ-ten.

Man.

in loving memory P. S. L.

13. Hymn: There is a green hill far away

Mrs Cecil Frances Alexander (1818–95)

'LEDGER'

66

14. The Crucifixion

John 19: 23–7

-mong them, and for my ves-ture they did cast lots. These things there-fore the sol-diers did.

Now there stood_ by the cross of Je - sus his mo-ther, and his

mo - ther's sis - ter,_____ Ma - ry the wife of Cle - o - phas, and

Ma - ry Mag - da - le - ne._____ When Je - sus there-fore saw his

mo - ther, and the dis - ci - ple stand-ing by, whom he loved, he saith un - to his mo - ther,

JESUS
mp espress.
EVANGELIST
p

Wo - man, wo - man, be - hold thy son! Then

mp espress.

Ped.

JESUS
mp espress.

saith he to the dis - ci - ple, Be - hold, be - hold___ thy

p
mp espress.

Man.
Ped.

dim.
p

mo - ther, thy mo - ther, mo - ther!

p

15. Meditation: Jesus, my Leman

13th-century English
adap. BC

*leman = loved one

if I know of love,

if I know of love,

if I know of love,

if I know of love,

if I know of love,

Man.

rit.

if I know of love.

if I know of love.

if I know of love.

if I know of love.

if I know of love.

rit.

Ped.

16. Jesus Dies on the Cross

John 19: 28–30

filled a sponge with vi-ne-gar, and put it u-pon hys-sop, and put it to his mouth. When Je-sus had re-ceived the vi-ne-gar, he said,

a little slower

JESUS It is fi-nished, fi-nished.

EVANGELIST And he

rit.

bowed his head, and gave up the ghost.

17. Hymn: When I survey the Wondrous Cross

Isaac Watts (1674–1748)

'AMELIA'

Processed in England by Enigma Music Production Services, Amersham, Bucks.
Printed in England by Halstan & Co. Ltd, Amersham, Bucks.

St John Passion

BOB CHILCOTT

PARTS 1 & 2 – TACET

(1. Sing, my tongue, the glorious battle; 2. The Garden; 3. Hymn: It is a thing most wonderful;
4. Peter's Denial; 5. Meditation: Miserere, my Maker; 6. Hymn: Drop, drop, slow tears; 7. The Judgment Hall (I);
8. Hymn: Jesu, grant me this, I pray; 9. Meditation: Christ, my Beloved; 10. The Judgment Hall (II); 11. Meditation: Away vain world)

PART 3

12. Jesus is Crucified

13. Hymn: There is a green hill far away – TACET

14. The Crucifixion

15. Meditation: Jesus, my Leman – TACET

16. Jesus Dies on the Cross